The Susan Jeffers Connection

by Will C. Howell

NO LONGER THE PROPERTY
OF THE
UNIVERSITY OF R. I. LIBRARY

FEARON TEACHER AIDS
Simon & Schuster Supplementary Education Group

Susan Jeffers,

I first met you through your books. Our second meeting was at Steven Kellogg's house. What a joy to finally meet, face to face, the creator of all those elegant Susan Jeffers books I had been sharing with children and teachers for so long. Thank you for trusting me to do this book.

Will Howell

Editor: Carol Williams
Copyeditor: Kristin Eclov
Illustration: Gwen Connelly
Cover illustration: Susan Jeffers
Design: Diann Abbott

Entire contents copyright © 1992 by Fearon Teacher Aids, part of the Education Group of Simon & Schuster, a Paramount Communications company. However, the individual purchaser may reproduce designated materials in this book for classroom and individual use, but the purchase of this book does not entitle reproduction of any part for an entire school, district, or system. Such use is strictly prohibited.

ISBN 0-86653-980-8

Printed in the United States of America
1. 9 8 7 6 5 4 3 2 1

Contents

Introduction 5

Meet Susan Jeffers 6

All the Pretty Horses 7
   Dream World Paragraphs 8

Baby Animals 9
   Animal Chart 10
   Waking Up 12

Benjamin's Barn 13
   Creative Writing 14
   Weighing the Barn 16
   Endangered Animals 18

Black Beauty 19
   A Day's Work 20
   Animal Work Force 22

Cinderella 23
   Point of View 24
   Telling Time 26

Close Your Eyes 29
   Descriptive Writing 30
   Literature Travel Brochures 31

Forest of Dreams 33
   Five Senses 34
   Butterflies 36

Hansel and Gretel 37
   Problem Solving 38
   Verb Vocabulary 39
   Which Bird? 40
   Creating Texture 42

Hiawatha 43
   Descriptive Writing 44
   Eastern Woodland Indians 45

If Wishes Were Horses 47
   Creative Writing 48
   Writing Classified Ads 49

The Midnight Farm 51
   Talking Numbers 52
   Drawing Farm Animals 54

Silent Night 57
   Dark and Light 58

The Snow Queen 61
   Properties of Water 62
   Crystal Palaces 64

Snow White and the Seven Dwarfs **65**
   Using the Yellow Pages 66
   Stranger Awareness 69

Stopping by Woods on a Snowy Evening **71**
   Adjective Snowflakes 72
   Snowflake Originals 74

The Three Jovial Huntsmen **77**
   Patterned Writing 78
   Hidden Pictures 80

Thumbelina **81**
   Miniature Magic 82
   Four Seasons 84
   Walnut Shell Art 86

Wild Robin **87**
   Creative Writing 88

The Wild Swans **89**
   Character Study 90
   Plants 92

Wynken, Blynken, and Nod **93**
   Night Writers 94

Introduction

The emphasis on "The Year of the Young Reader" (1989), "International Literacy Year" (1990), and "The Year of the Lifetime Reader" (1991) has helped children's literature come of age. Research confirms that good reading and writing are best taught by using good books. And today, educators are fortunate to have a wide selection of excellent children's books to choose from.

The Susan Jeffers Connection is written for librarians and teachers who want to effectively use good literature in their classrooms. The lessons present art, math, creative writing, science, and social studies activities to accompany books by this one outstanding author/illustrator. The variety of interdisciplinary activities and the whole-language instructional approach incorporated in the lessons will help you meet the diverse needs and interests of your students.

As students become familiar with various works by a single author/illustrator, they develop an ability to analyze literary and artistic style. Children can go to the library and select books written or illustrated by authors they feel as if they have actually met. "Connecting" with authors stimulates students to become involved in and enthusiastic about reading, writing, and learning. *The Susan Jeffers Connection* gives students the opportunity to meet an author/illustrator whose books are fine art collections between the covers.

Lessons require minimal preparation, while resulting in maximum participation and learning. A brief synopsis of each book is included. Read the book aloud to the children and invite them to enjoy the illustrations before participating in the activities. Exciting activities, including making crystal ice palaces, creating adjective snowstorms, and designing travel brochures, will help you to enhance and reinforce your curriculum.

Meet Susan Jeffers

Susan Jeffers was born on October 7, 1942.

As a young girl, Susan was instructed and encouraged in art by her mother. Her mother taught her how to really look at what was around her. She spent hours teaching Susan how to make objects appear round or flat and she showed Susan how to mix paint. Most of all, Susan recalls that her mother gave her a "feeling of immense joy" in her work.

Susan's art "career" began when she was a student in a small New Jersey elementary school. She was asked by her teacher to paint a historic mural of ancient Egypt. Susan suspects that she was chosen as much for her ability to paint without dripping as for her talent. However, this careful precision and creativity have stayed with her.

After graduating from The Pratt Institute in 1964, Susan went to work for various publishing houses. She repaired type, pasted up illustrations, and designed books and book jackets. Her experience gave her a good sense of how a book is made.

In 1968, Susan opened her own studio with artist friend, Rosemary Wells. She also began her first book, *The Buried Moon*. This book was published, received excellent reviews, and started Susan on a successful writing career. Susan's second book, *The Three Jovial Huntsmen,* took her three years to complete. Discouraged by the rejection of her first version, she put the book away for a while. When she returned to the project, Susan reworked the entire book. Her efforts paid off because in 1974, Susan received a Caldecott Honor for *The Three Jovial Huntsmen.*

Susan Jeffers loves the outdoors, painting, horseback riding, and good friends—all of which show through in her work. Her books are filled with delicious detail from nature, grand horses running across the pages, and the warmth and strength of human relationships. Her love of painting shows in the exquisite execution of each page. Truly the "feeling of immense joy" in her work overflows to the reader.

All the Pretty Horses

A lover of horses, Susan Jeffers entices readers to join her reverie. Her exquisite drawings give fresh interpretation to this familiar lullaby.

New York: Macmillan, 1974

DREAM WORLD PARAGRAPHS

Materials:

- lined paper
- pencils

Lesson Procedure

1. In this lullaby, pretty little horses are promised to be present when the sleeper awakens from dreaming. Ask children what they hope will be waiting for them when they wake up from a dream.
2. Encourage students to write down their dream-world thoughts in well-written paragraphs. Remind students of several of the elements of a complete paragraph, including a topic sentence, several supporting sentences that add description or explanation, and a closing sentence that restates the topic.
3. Sample topic sentence starters might include:

   When I woke up, I was surrounded by . . .
   The last sleepy thought I remember before I drifted off to a world of dreams was . . .
   My dream turned to reality when I noticed . . .

Taking It Further . . .

Point out the four types of horses that are mentioned in the story (blacks, bays, dapples, and grays). Suggest other categories to students, such as apples, dogs, or sports. Challenge students to name at least four items in each category.

All the Pretty Horses

Baby Animals

How do animals wake up in the morning? What do they have for lunch? Where do they sleep at night? The charming words and illustrations in this story explore the wonders of farm life.

Written by Margaret Wise Brown
New York: Random House, 1989

ANIMAL CHART

Materials:

- worksheet on page 11
- pencils

Lesson Procedure

1. Compare and contrast the habits, diets, and behaviors of the farm animals mentioned in the story.
2. Give students the worksheet and encourage them to fill in the chart recalling how the little girl and each of the animals moved in the morning, ate at lunch, and slept at night.
3. Invite students to complete the last two sections of the worksheet by thinking of two other animals and listing their behaviors in each column.

Taking It Further . . .

Invite students to write paragraphs or short stories describing the way they get up in the morning, what they eat for lunch, and what they do to prepare for bed at night.

Name _____

It's All in a Day

Animal	Move in the Morning	Eat for Lunch	Sleep at Night
BIRD			
HORSE			
PIG			
LAMB			
CAT			
DOG			
GIRL			

Baby Animals

Materials:

- lined paper
- pencils

Lesson Procedure

1. Discuss ways the author uses the senses to describe the morning as each animal wakes up.

    the bird saw soft gray light
    the little horse felt the warm sun
    the mother dog began to lick her puppies
    the mother dog sniffed the morning air
    one little kitten began to purr
    one little puppy barked

2. Stimulate a discussion about how students would describe their typical morning using information from each of their five senses. Ask students what they first see when they open their eyes in the morning or what sounds they first hear.
3. Give each student a sheet of lined paper. Ask students to make five columns on the paper and label each column with one of the five senses (see, touch, taste, hear, smell).
4. Encourage students to take the paper home and make a list under each heading describing their mornings.
5. When students return the next day with their lists, invite them to write descriptive paragraphs about their mornings using the information they have gathered.

Taking It Further . . .

Challenge students to write paragraphs about their lunch describing the textures, tastes, and feel of the food. Or, invite students to create bedtime tales describing the mood, sights, and sounds around them at night.

Benjamin's Barn

Oh, to have a barn of your very own and to fill it with horses, sheep, cows, elephants, pterodactyls, and pirate ships! That is just what Reeve Lindbergh and Susan Jeffers have done in this enormously happy book.

Written by Reeve Lindbergh
New York: Dial, 1990

Materials:

- worksheet on page 15
- pencils

Lesson Procedure

1. Encourage students to name all the items Benjamin used to fill his barn. List the items on the chalkboard.

elephant	pigeon	king, queen, and guests
sheep	princess	cow and bull
pirate ship	raccoon	rhinoceros
horse	brass band	billy goat
pterodactyl	geese	

2. Ask students which items on the list they would include if they had a barn to fill. Encourage students to add their own imaginative ideas.
3. Give each student a worksheet and write his or her name on the blank in the title. Challenge students to fill their barns with real and imaginative items listing them on the lines provided. Or, delete the lines from the worksheet before duplicating and have students draw the items that would fill their barns.

Taking It Further . . .

Invite students to use their lists to write original poetry. Encourage students to think of adjectives to describe the barn following the pattern provided in the story. For example, Benjamin knew a frail princess could sleep in the trough because the barn was enormously *soft*. Benjamin could keep a pterodactyl inside because the barn was enormously *wide*.

Name _____

_____'s Barn

Use your imagination to fill your barn!

WEIGHING THE BARN

Materials:

- worksheet on page 17
- pencils
- calculators (optional)

Lesson Procedure

1. Ask students to recall each item in Benjamin's barn and make a list on the chalkboard.
2. Encourage students to guess the weight of each item and write the number beside the item on the chalkboard.
3. After guesses are recorded, use the information on the worksheet to give students the accurate weight for each item.
4. Explain to students that the barn will hold 10,000 pounds. Since a pirate ship would probably weigh over 150 tons (300,000 pounds), it would not likely fit in a barn. However, a husky 220-pound pirate would.
5. Invite students to name combinations of items on the list in which the combined weight total is equal to or less than 10,000 pounds.
6. Students may use the worksheet to compute their combinations.

Taking It Further . . .

Using the same item weights, give students a new weight limit for the barn. Ask students to remove or add to their combinations so they meet the new weight limit requirement.

Benjamin's Barn

Name _____

Benjamin's Barn

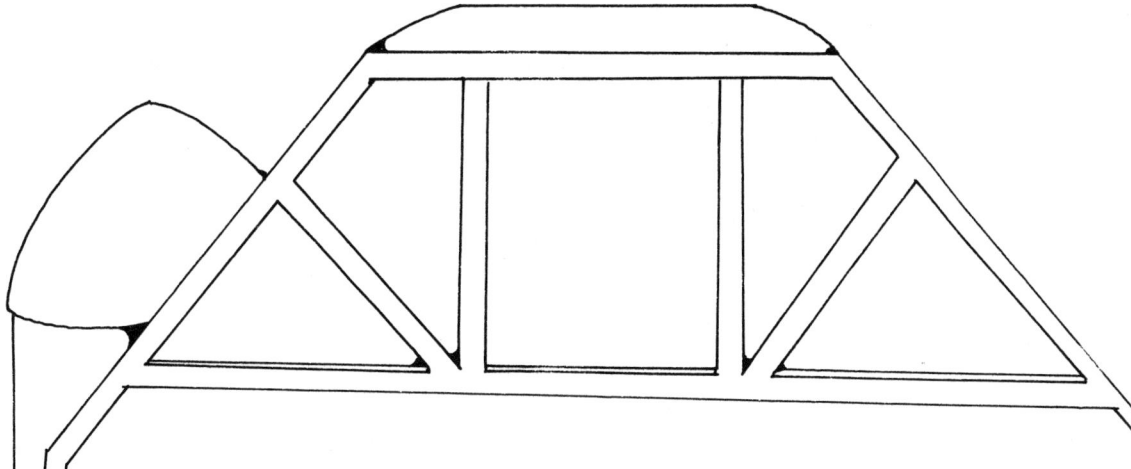

If the barn holds 10,000 pounds, what combinations of items could be put in the barn without exceeding the weight limit?

elephant	10,000 lbs	brass band	
sheep	200 lbs	(4 men)	700 lbs
pirate	220 lbs	goose	25 lbs
horse	1,000 lbs	king	175 lbs
pterodactyl	100 lbs	queen	130 lbs
pigeon	1 lb	cow	1,500 lbs
princess	125 lbs	bull	2,000 lbs
raccoon	20 lbs	rhinoceros	5,000 lbs
billy goat	150 lbs		

Example:

rhinoceros	5,000 lbs
two bulls	4,000 lbs
horse	1,000 lbs
TOTAL:	**10,000 lbs**

ENDANGERED ANIMALS

Materials:

- lined paper
- construction paper
- scissors
- pencils
- crayons or markers

Lesson Procedure

1. Benjamin chose to fill his barn with many items, including a rhinoceros and an elephant. Both of these animals are considered endangered. Discuss with students the meaning of the word *endangered*. Then have students brainstorm a list of other endangered animals.
2. Provide students with a partial list of endangered animals. Encourage students to compare and add to their own lists.

Bengal tiger	mountain gorilla	California condor	rhinoceros
humpback whale	green sea turtle	wallaby	elephant
orangutan			

3. Individually or in pairs, encourage students to choose an endangered animal and write a brief report about it. Ask students to include a brief description of the animal, where it lives, why it is in danger of becoming extinct, and what is being done to protect the animal.
4. Students can use construction paper for drawings of their endangered animal and its habitat.
5. Make an endangered animal bulletin board to display the student's reports and drawings. Choose one group to create a habitat for their endangered animal as the background for the bulletin board.

Taking It Further . . .

Students will enjoy comparing their work with the book *Hey! Get Off Our Train* by John Burningham (New York: Crown, 1989).

Black Beauty

From the compelling portrait to the joyous final pages, Susan Jeffers has captured Black Beauty with singular power and grace. The splendid illustrations, combined with Robin McKinley's superb story, provide a version of this classic for everyone to enjoy.

Written by Anna Sewell and adapted by Robin McKinley
New York: Random House, 1986

A DAY'S WORK

Materials:

- worksheet on page 21
- pencils
- calculators (optional)

Lesson Procedure

1. In the 1800s, horses played a major role in transportation and in accomplishing the tasks in a day's work. Black Beauty came in contact with many people throughout her life. These people mastered over her, cared for her, or needed her help to accomplish a task. Ask children to recall the people in the story whose jobs related to caring for or using horses.

   blacksmith   groom   grain dealer
   coachman   farrier

2. Encourage children to provide a description of each job.

   blacksmith—forge iron, make horseshoes
   coachman—drive a carriage (often for aristocracy)
   groom—feed and condition horses and clean stables
   farrier—shoe horses and look after the care of the horse's feet
   grain dealer—sell and deliver feed for livestock and poultry

3. Have students complete the worksheet by calculating each story problem.

   Worksheet Answer Key
   1. $30.00
   2. $37.50
   3. $400.00
   4. $1,375.00

Taking It Further . . .

Horses have played important and interesting roles throughout history. Encourage students to select topics of interest and report on various ways horses have been important in battle, recreation, and work.

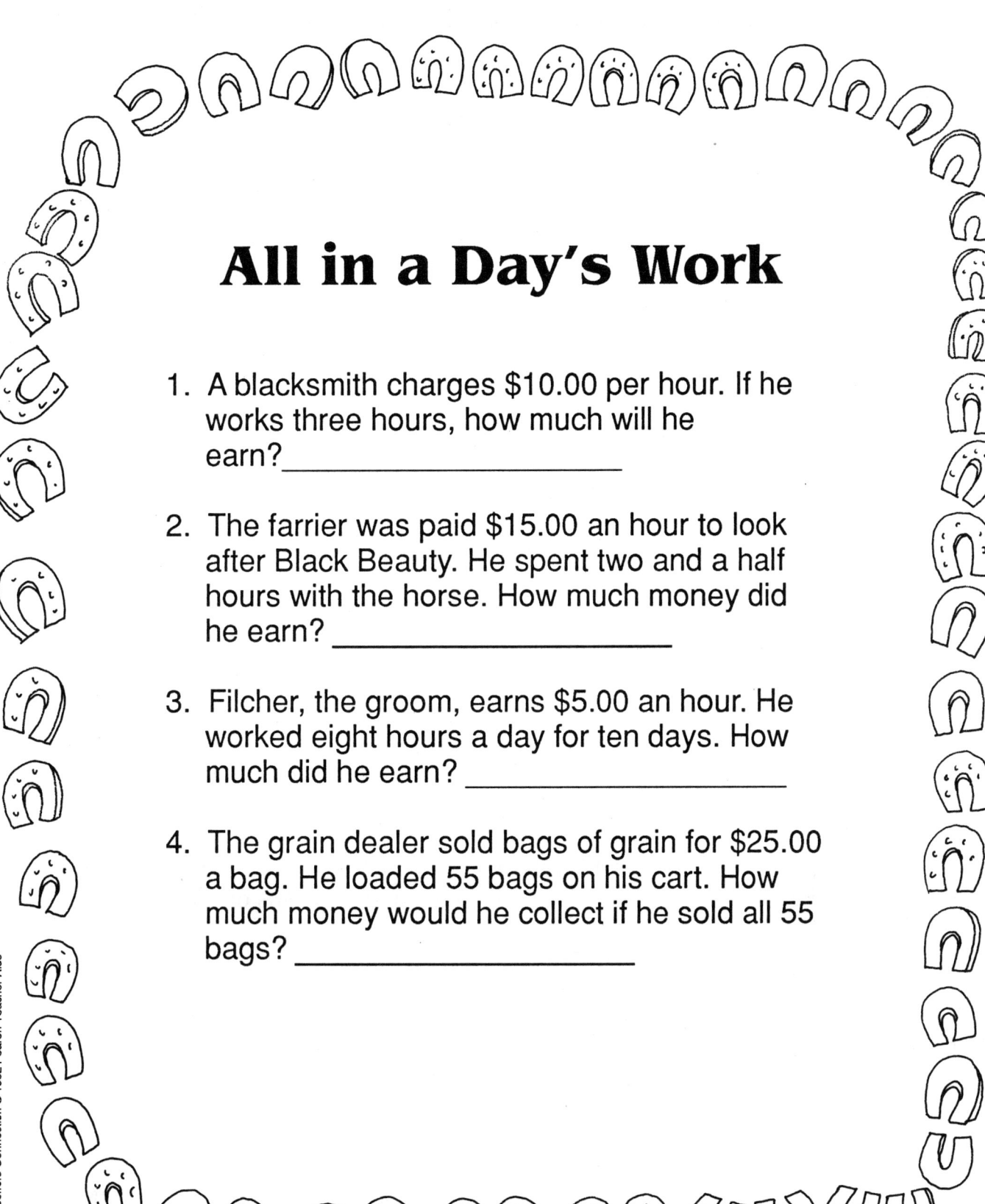

Name _____

All in a Day's Work

1. A blacksmith charges $10.00 per hour. If he works three hours, how much will he earn? _____

2. The farrier was paid $15.00 an hour to look after Black Beauty. He spent two and a half hours with the horse. How much money did he earn? _____

3. Filcher, the groom, earns $5.00 an hour. He worked eight hours a day for ten days. How much did he earn? _____

4. The grain dealer sold bags of grain for $25.00 a bag. He loaded 55 bags on his cart. How much money would he collect if he sold all 55 bags? _____

Black Beauty

21

ANIMAL WORK FORCE

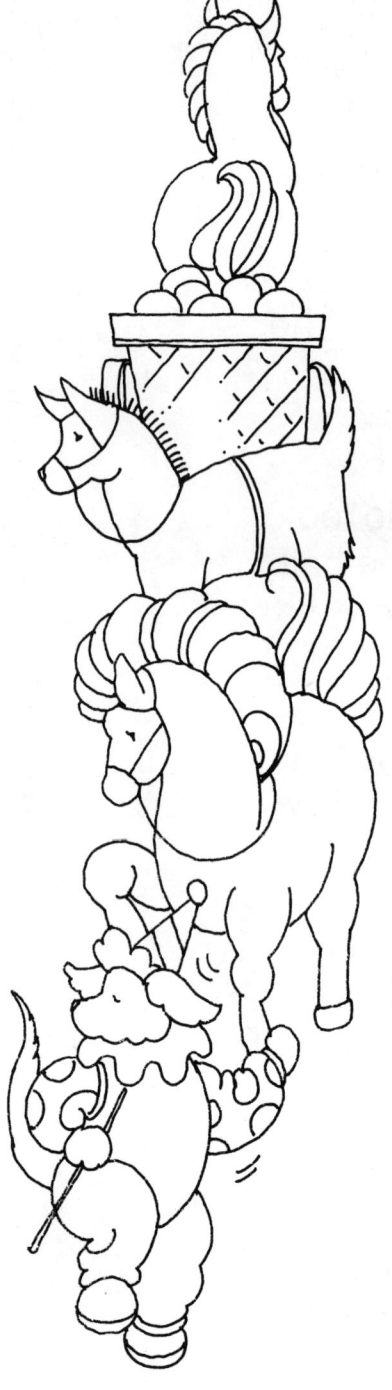

Materials:

- lined paper
- pencils
- encyclopedias

Lesson Procedure

1. Discuss different ways horses work for people, such as in hunting, riding, pulling carriages, and pulling wagons.
2. Challenge children to think of other animals that help people, too. Make a list of the animals. Your list might include:

guide dogs	police dogs
carrier pigeons	performing animals
hunting dogs	

3. Encourage students to choose an animal that helps people and use encyclopedias to find information about that animal. Invite students to write a few paragraphs or a short report about their findings.
4. Invite students to share their reports orally with the class.

Taking It Further . . .

After students have completed their reports, encourage each student to write a story about the animal's life. Encourage the students to write the stories from the animal's point of view, just as Black Beauty was written from the horse's point of view.

Black Beauty

Cinderella

This well-loved fairy tale is brought to life by Susan Jeffers' enchanting illustrations. With the faces so fair, the costumes so elegant, and the palace so splendid, the reader is magically swept into a romantic kingdom.

Written by Charles Perrault and retold by Amy Ehrlich
New York: Dial, 1985

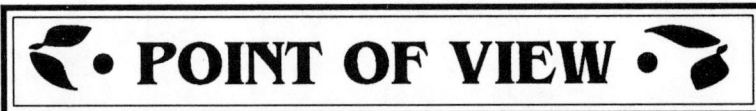

POINT OF VIEW

Materials:

- worksheet on page 25
- pencils

Lesson Procedure

1. Discuss the point of view from which this version of Cinderella is told—a third person tells the story from an outsider's perspective.
2. Encourage children to think of other perspectives from which the story could be told. Make a list of different points of view on the chalkboard. Some story titles might include:

    Cinderella's Foot Has a Story to Tell
    Straight from the Horse's Mouth
    Cinderella's Broom Tells All
    It's Not Easy Being a Fairy Godmother
    My Life As a Mouse and a Horse!

3. Give each student a copy of the worksheet on page 25. Invite children to choose a point of view and write an original version of Cinderella from that perspective.

Taking It Further . . .

Compare different versions of Cinderella.

Clark, Ann Nolan. *In the Land of Small Dragons*. New York: Viking, 1979.
Climo, Shirley. *The Egyptian Cinderella*. New York: Crowell, 1989.
Hooks, William H. *Moss Gown*. New York: Clarion, 1987.
Steel, Flora Annie Webster. *Tattercoats*. Scarsdale, New York: Bradbury, 1976.
Louie, Ai-Ling. *Yeh-Shen: A Cinderella Story from China*. New York: Philomel, 1982.

Name _____

Cinderella

• TELLING TIME •

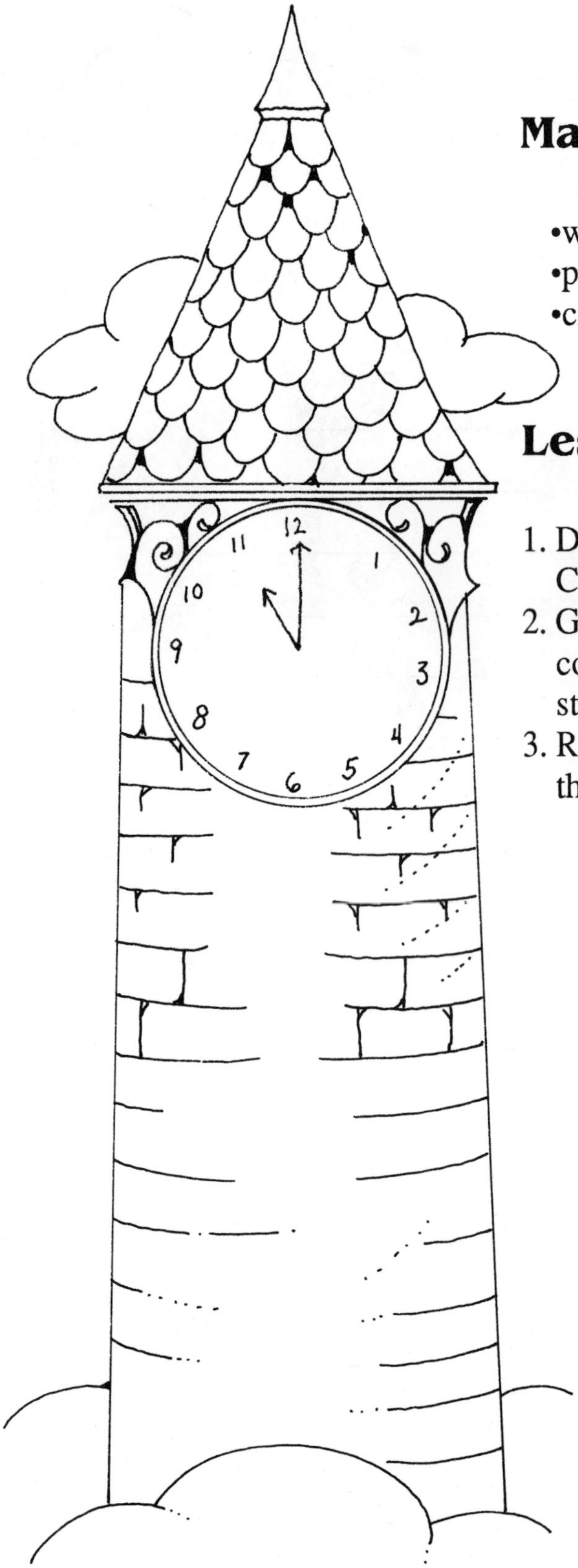

Materials:

- worksheet on page 28
- pencils
- crayons or markers

Lesson Procedure

1. Discuss the importance time played in the story of Cinderella.
2. Give students a worksheet and explain that they will be coloring the clocks to show what time the events in the story might have taken place.
3. Read the following directions aloud to students, giving them time to color or mark their worksheets.

   1. Draw hands on the tower clock to show what time Cinderella was supposed to leave the ball.

   2. The stepsisters left for the ball at 6:00. Find the clock that shows what time the stepsisters left. Color it red (C).

   3. Cinderella's fairy godmother appeared at 15 minutes after 6:00. Find the clock that shows what time the fairy godmother appeared. Draw a black circle around it (H).

   4. At 6:30, a pumpkin was turned into a coach. Find the clock that says 6:30. Color it purple (B).

   5. At 6:45, the fairy godmother turned six white mice into horses. Find the clock that shows what time the horses appeared. Draw a green line under it (F).

   6. At 7:00, a rat became a coachman. Find the clock that says 7:00. Color it blue (J).

26 *Cinderella*

7. At 7:15, six lizards turned into six footmen. Find the clock that says 7:15. Draw a yellow square around it (D).

8. At 7:30, the fairy godmother made Cinderella a beautiful gown for the ball. Find the clock that says 7:30. Color it green (I).

9. Cinderella arrived at the ball at 8:00. Find the clock that says 8:00. Color it yellow (A).

10. Cinderella danced with the prince until 11:00. Find the clock that says 11:00. Draw a red square around it (G).

11. At a quarter to twelve, Cindrella left the ball. Find the clock that says a quarter to twelve. Draw a black triangle around it. (E)

Taking It Further . . .

Make a display of several pumpkins of various sizes, or invite students to bring in some pumpkins. Weigh the pumpkins and measure their circumference. Graph the results. Cinderella's pumpkin turned into a carriage. Invite students to write stories about what they would like their pumpkins to become.

Name _____

Telling Time

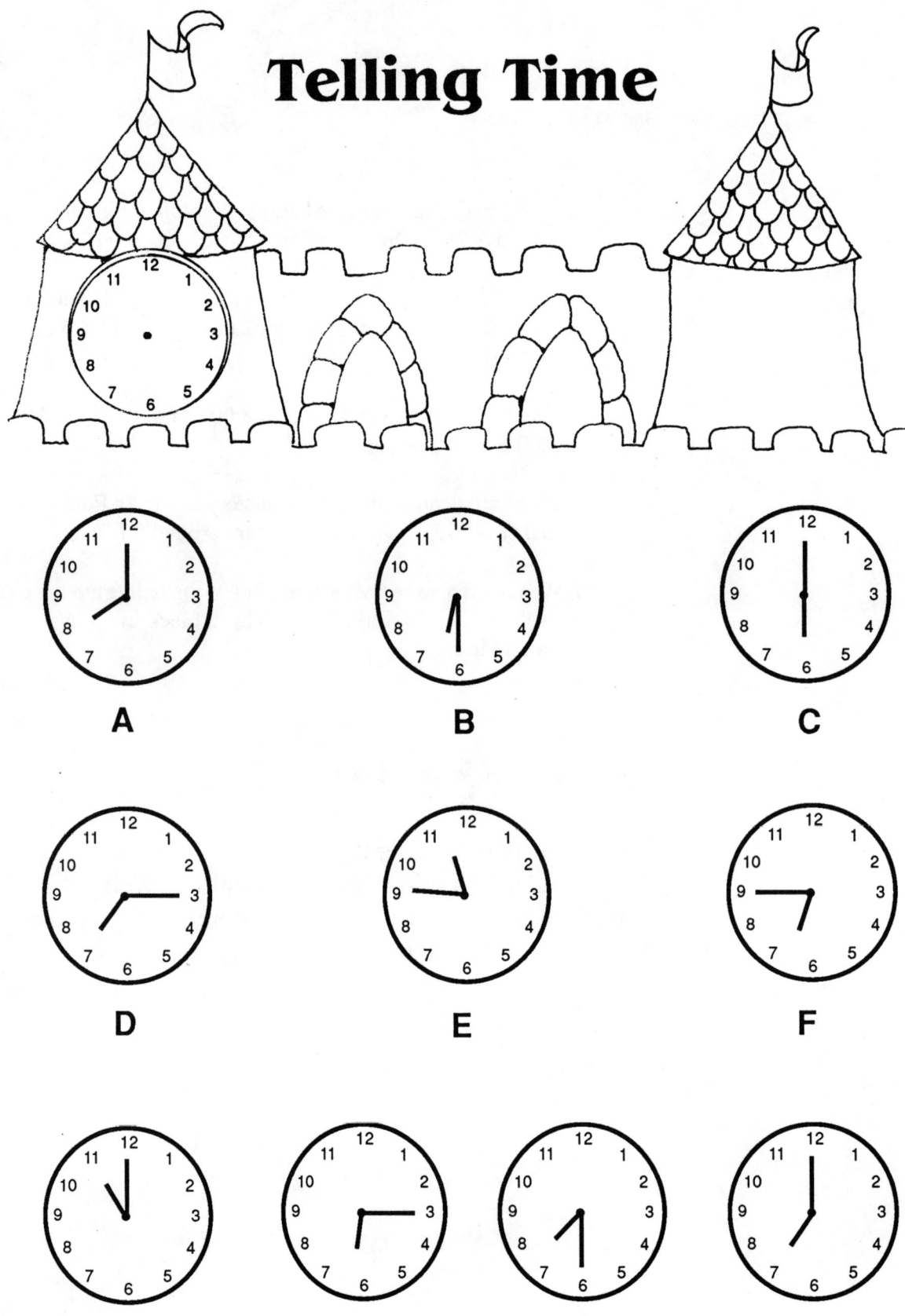

28　　*Cinderella*

Close Your Eyes

"Close your eyes and you can be..." anywhere you would like to be. Jean Marzollo's soft, flowing words sweep the reader away to peaceful places. Susan Jeffers' illustrations provide a tranquility that tucks this lullaby into those last sleepy thoughts.

Written by Jean Marzollo
New York: Dial, 1978

DESCRIPTIVE WRITING

Materials:

- lined paper
- pencils

Lesson Procedure

1. Point out to students how the author of the story suggests that by closing your eyes, you can be anywhere you want to be.
2. Create a quiet, peaceful atmosphere in the classroom by turning off the lights and playing soft background music. You might even light a scented candle or use fragrant potpourri to add to the mood.
3. Invite students to close their eyes and imagine a place they would like to be. As students are thinking, quietly ask the following questions:

   What kinds of things can you see in the place you are thinking of?
   What can you smell?
   What can you hear?
   What can you feel?

4. Write the questions on the chalkboard. Encourage students to open their eyes and review the questions. Then have the students write down their feelings, descriptions, and thoughts about their special place.
5. Help students organize their thoughts into well-written descriptive paragraphs.
6. Invite students to illustrate their descriptive paragraphs.

Taking It Further . . .

Invite students to imagine visiting another country. Have students write a description of what they think they would find there. Encourage students to use encyclopedias to verify or adjust their impressions.

LITERATURE TRAVEL BROCHURES

Materials:

- drawing paper
- lined paper
- pencils
- crayons or markers

Lesson Procedure

1. Explain to students that reading a book is another way of "traveling" to another place. Invite students to share places they have "visited" through books.
2. Have each student select a book they have enjoyed reading. Have students make a descriptive list of things they saw, felt, heard, and touched by reading about the setting where the story took place.
3. Invite each student to fold a sheet of drawing paper into thirds to make a literature travel brochure describing some of the sights and sounds experienced in the book. Encourage students to illustrate their literature travel brochures to entice others to read the books, too. Be sure students include the title of the book, author, illustrator, and setting description.

Taking It Further . . .

Display the brochures on a bulletin board entitled "Books Take You Places."

Close Your Eyes

Forest of Dreams

A child rejoices in the coming of spring. She celebrates her own senses that enable her to experience the excitement of the changing world. She moves from sight to touch to sound with irresistible exaltation. As the young girl revels in her harmony with nature, so the reader revels in the harmony of the text and the illustration.

Written by Rosemary Wells
New York: Dial, 1988

FIVE SENSES

Materials:

- worksheet on page 35
- pencils

Lesson Procedure

1. Discuss how the author uses the senses of sight, touch, and sound to describe nature's gifts. Invite children to help compile a list of the marvels of nature described in the book.
2. Encourage children to categorize the items in the list according to the sense the young girl used to experience each one.

Sight	Touch	Sound
woods and all who live within it	ice	stream
	tree	
winter sun	rain	

3. Give each child a copy of the worksheet. Encourage children to list some of nature's gifts that they enjoy seeing, hearing, touching, smelling, or tasting. Emphasize the use of descriptive words, such as *prickly* trees or *whispering* streams.

Taking It Further . . .

Divide the class into five groups. Assign each group one of the five senses (touch, taste, smell, hearing, sight). Invite groups to illustrate, on a large mural, what they are able to enjoy through their senses.

Forest of Dreams

Name _____

Nature's Gifts

Make a list of some of nature's gifts that you enjoy seeing, smelling, hearing, tasting, and touching.

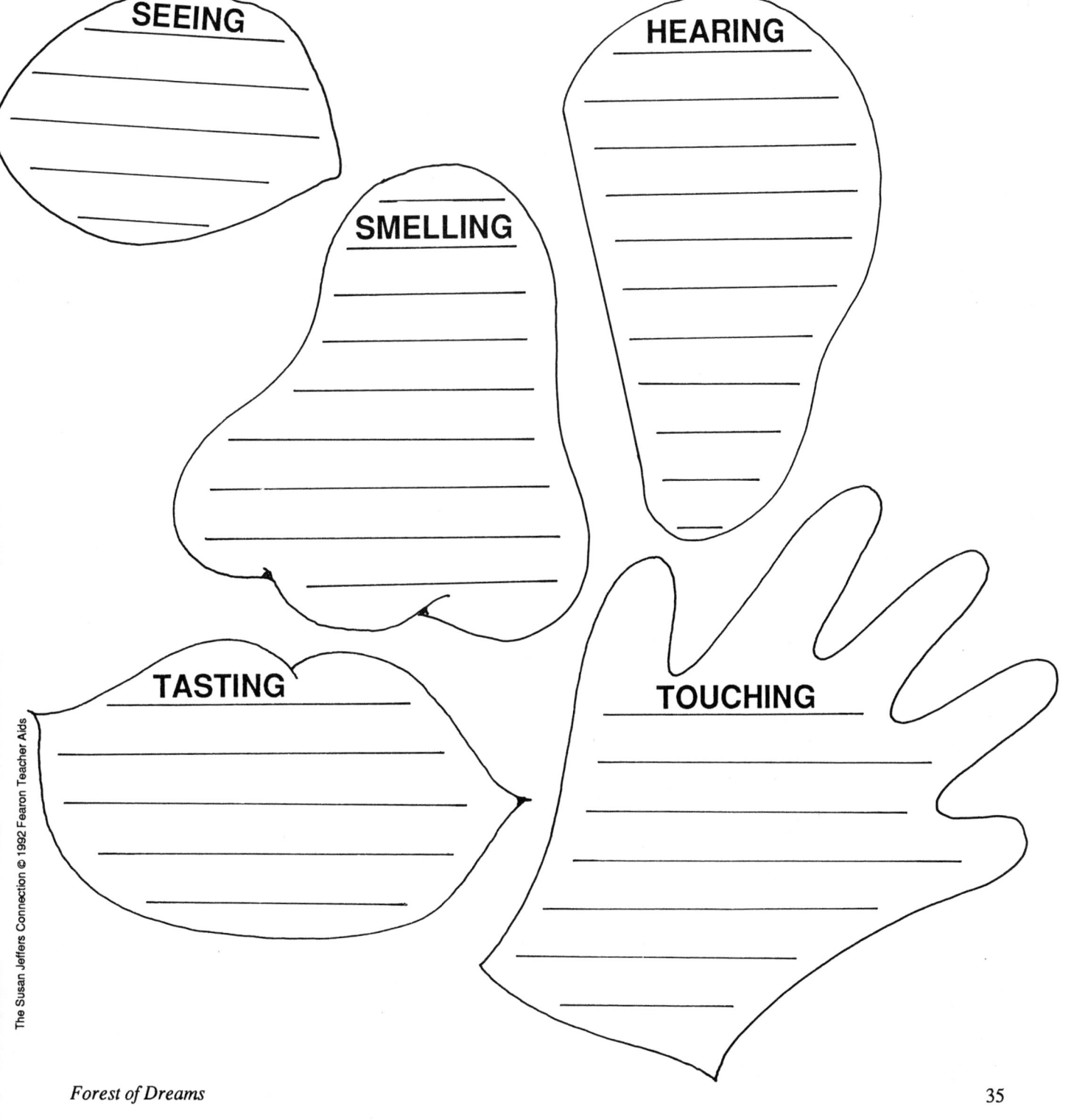

Forest of Dreams

35

Materials:

- lined paper
- drawing paper
- pencils
- encyclopedias and reference books
- crayons, colored pencils, or markers

Lesson Procedure

1. Show children the last page of the story and invite them to carefully examine the butterflies illustrated. Ask students if they can identify any of the butterflies by name. Students might be most familiar with the Monarch butterfly in the foreground on the right-hand page.
2. Divide the class into research groups of 3-5 students. Direct each group to select a butterfly from the last page of the story or from an encyclopedia on which to write a report.
3. Encourage groups to use encyclopedias and other reference books to find out information about their butterfly's food source and eating habits, environment, migration, hibernation, protection, and life cycle.
4. Invite each group to make a large and detailed drawing of their butterflies on drawing paper.
5. Bind all the butterfly reports and illustrations into a class book.

Taking It Further . . .

Students can design charts illustrating the life cycle of a butterfly, including the egg, larva (caterpillar), pupa (chrysalis), and adult butterfly. Or, students can draw diagrams illustrating butterfly parts, such as the wings, veins, antennae, compound eye, proboscis, thorax, and abdomen.

Forest of Dreams

Hansel and Gretel

Susan Jeffers has created a beautiful rendition of this favorite children's classic. Her illustrations are majestic, full of awe and power, yet tempered with delicate lines and gentle color. Ms. Jeffers has masterfully blended elements of evil and fear with those of hope and strength.

Written by the Brothers Grimm
New York: Dial, 1980

• PROBLEM SOLVING •

Materials:

- 4" x 6" file cards
- pencils

Lesson Procedure

1. Discuss the inventive methods Hansel and Gretel used to solve their problem in the forest (leaving a trail of white pebbles and bread crumbs).
2. Discuss how each method was either a success or a failure and why (pebbles left a reliable trail, but bread crumbs were eaten by birds).
3. Encourage children to put themselves in Hansel and Gretel's place and think of alternate methods for providing a safe return home from the forest. Ideas might include following a river, tying a piece of bright clothing to a tree, or cutting small notches into trees along the way. Discuss whether the new methods would be successful or not.
4. Give each student a 4" x 6" card to write down a solution to Hansel and Gretel's problem.
5. Have students trade cards. Students can read the solution cards and write comments or questions on the back about possible outcomes.
6. Divide the class into groups of 4-6 students. Encourage students to collaborate and agree upon the best solution for helping Hansel and Gretel solve their problem. Invite groups to share their results with the class.

Taking It Further . . .

Taking the story more seriously, encourage students to write a list of ways to deal with family problems. Ideas might include telling parents how you feel or talking to an adult you trust.

VERB VOCABULARY

Materials:

- lined paper
- pencils

Lesson Procedure

1. Write a list of descriptive verbs used in the story.

glitter	swoop	murmur
console	hobble	shriek
crumble	creep	desert
blaze	snare	howl

2. Have students copy the list on lined paper leaving several empty lines between each word.
3. Ask students to write definitions from context for each verb and then use each word in a sentence.
4. Invite students to read their best sentences aloud to the class, omitting the verb. Encourage classmates to guess the missing word.

Taking It Further . . .

Challenge students to write original stories using as many of the verbs in the list as possible.

Hansel and Gretel

WHICH BIRD?

Materials:

- worksheet on page 41
- pencils
- encyclopedias and reference books

Lesson Procedure

1. Invite children to look again at the many beautiful pictures of birds throughout the story (owl, dove, duck).
2. Discuss how the birds look different—including their eyes, wings, bills, and feet. Discuss purposes for the differences, such as food gathering, protection, and adapting to environment.
3. Give students a copy of the worksheet and invite them to match the illustrations with the descriptions.
4. Discuss the worksheet answers, inviting student participation and comments.

Worksheet Answer Key

cracking, 3	grasping and tearing, 3
picking, 2	perching, 1
scooping, 1	swimming, 2

5. Encourage children to name a bird that has each type of bill or foot.

bill for cracking—parrot	feet for tearing—owl
bill for picking—robin	feet for perching—dove
bill for scooping—pelican	feet for swimming—duck

Taking It Further . . .

Invite each student to choose a bird and write a report, including information such as the bird's food source and feeding habits, wing type, protection, and environment.

Hansel and Gretel

Name _____

Bills and Feet

Match each picture with its description by writing the correct number on each line.

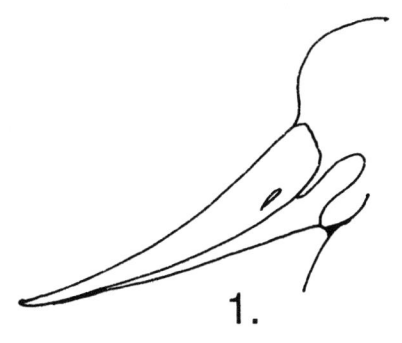

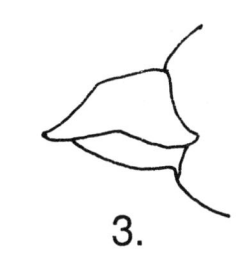

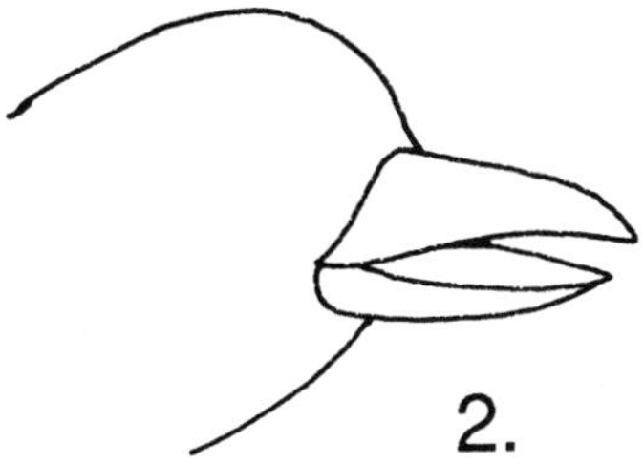

Which bill is used for

cracking? _____
picking? _____
scooping? _____

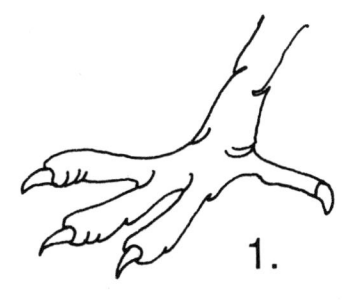

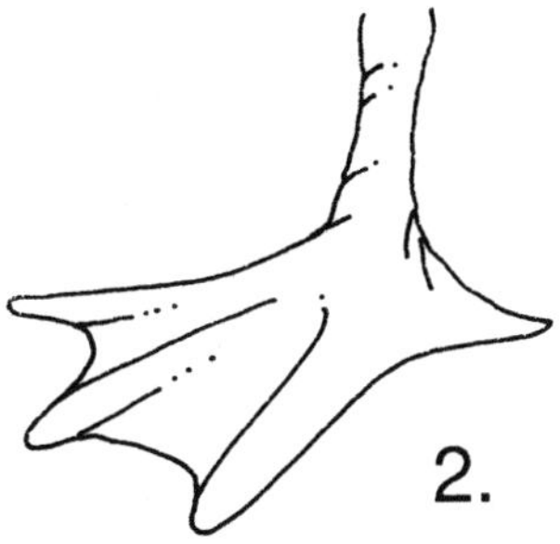

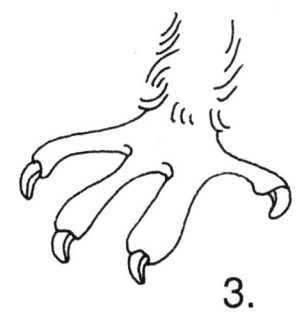

Which foot is used for

grasping and tearing? _____
perching? _____
swimming? _____

Hansel and Gretel

41

CREATING TEXTURE

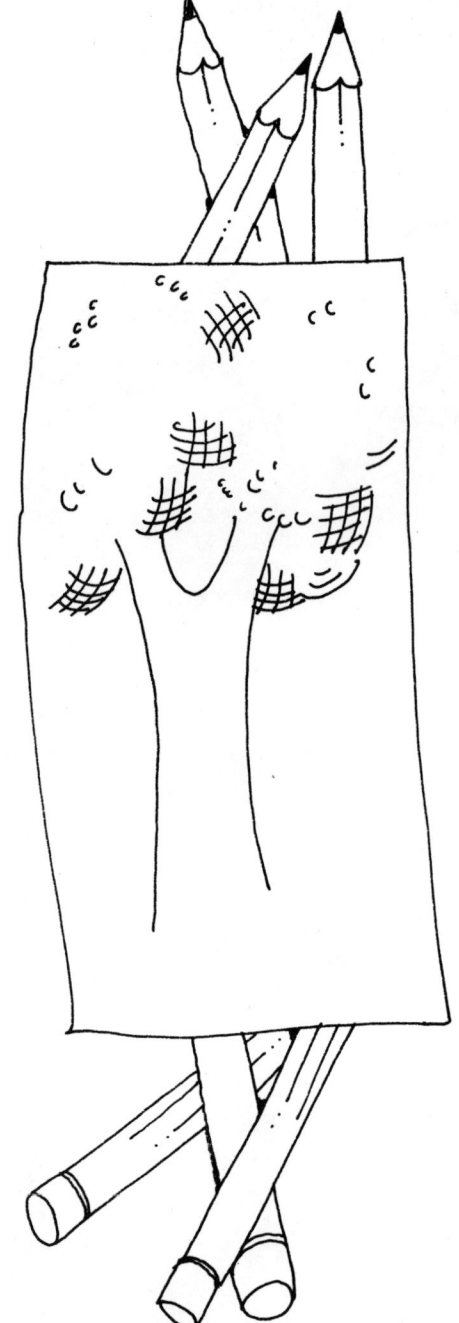

Materials:

- drawing paper
- pencils

Lesson Procedure

1. Invite children to take a closer look at Susan Jeffers' illustrations throughout the story. Point out the illustrator's use of tiny circles and hatch lines used to create texture. For example, on the title page, there are tiny circles in the trees and hatch lines in the sky. On the gingerbread house, there are hatch lines on the trees and in the grass.
2. Encourage students to try these techniques to create a textured illustration. Have students select a subject to draw, such as an outdoor scene, a stuffed animal, a floral arrangement, or a still-life display.
3. After students draw the outline of the design, invite them to add texture by filling in their shapes with tiny circles, hatch lines, or by using another technique of their choosing.

Taking It Further . . .

Discuss Susan Jeffers' use of pastel colors to create softness and gentleness in her illustrations. Encourage students to enhance their pictures using pastel colors.

Hansel and Gretel

Hiawatha

The striking cover portrait of Hiawatha begins the journey as the reader turns the pages and is transported to the famous "shores of Gitche Gumee." This well-known portion of Longfellow's epic poem is captured with a majesty that perfectly fits the grandeur of the words.

Written by Henry Wadsworth Longfellow
New York: Dial, 1983

DESCRIPTIVE WRITING

Materials:

- drawing paper
- lined paper
- pencils
- nature prints (landscapes, seascapes, forests)

Lesson Procedure

1. Read the first two pages of the story without showing children the illustrations. Ask children to create mental images in their minds as they listen to the words.
2. Reread the first two pages and have children draw the mental images that come to mind when they hear the words a second time.
3. Show children Susan Jeffers' interpretation of the passage. Explain to children that they will have an opportunity to paint a picture with words.
4. Give each student a nature print. Challenge students to write descriptive poems or paragraphs about their scenes. Encourage students to describe their pictures using all five of their senses. Emphasize the use of similes, metaphors, and descriptive adjectives.

Taking It Further . . .

Display the nature prints randomly on a bulletin board. Post the student descriptions randomly as well. Invite students to read the descriptions and match them to the scenes they describe.

Hiawatha

EASTERN WOODLAND INDIANS

Materials:

- worksheet on page 46
- lined paper
- butcher paper
- crayons or markers
- pencils
- encyclopedias and reference books

Lesson Procedure

1. Give each student a copy of the worksheet. Read the background information together and discuss some of the characteristics of Eastern Woodland Indians.
2. Have students work in pairs or small groups to find out additional information about this group of Native Americans.
3. Divide the class into six groups to make a culturally accurate mural depicting the Eastern Woodland Indian way of life. Each group can illustrate one of the six categories outlined on the worksheet.

Taking It Further . . .

Assign study groups of 4-6 students to research and compare other Native American groups: Northwest Coast, Arctic, California, Columbia Plateau, Great Basin, Southwest, and Plains.

Hiawatha

Name _____

Eastern Woodland Indians

Hiawatha captures the lifestyle and values of the Indians of the Eastern Woodlands. These Native Americans dwelt under a canopy of deciduous trees and conifers, surrounded by lakes, rivers, and the Atlantic ocean. They were accustomed to extreme weather, ranging from frozen winters to steaming hot summers.

The Indians of this region enjoyed a rich, varied diet, which they acquired by hunting, gathering, fishing, and planting. Their homes were dome-shaped wigwams covered with birch bark. Birch bark was also used to make canoes. Clothing was made from deerskin.

What additional information can you discover about the people of the Eastern Woodlands? Locate some interesting facts for each category listed below.

Natural Environment
_____
_____

Cultural Environment (rules, recreation, religion, art)
_____
_____

Food
_____
_____

Shelter
_____
_____

Clothing
_____
_____

Travel
_____
_____

Hiawatha

If Wishes Were Horses

Wishes come true for young horse enthusiasts in this splendid read-aloud book for all ages. A jovial collection of Mother Goose nursery rhymes parades through the pages. Susan Jeffers has provided her own whimsical interpretation of her favorite rhymes about horses.

New York: Dutton, 1979

• CREATIVE WRITING •

Materials:

- lined paper
- pencils

Lesson Procedure

1. Ask children to recall some of the adventures the characters in the rhymes had with their horses.

    Charlie rides his horse to visit his grandmother.
    A group of gentlemen enjoy jumping over fences and scrambling down ditches on their horses in pursuit of a fox.
    Annie chooses a galloping horse and rides it until she can ride no more.

2. Ask children to name an animal they would wish for if they were guaranteed the wish would be granted.
3. Encourage children to imagine real or fantasy adventures they could share with their new pet. For example, children may dream of taking first prize in a pet show, owning the largest rabbit in the world, or sailing the seas on the back of their pet whale.
4. Have students write a paragraph, short story, or even a poem about themselves and their fantasy pet entitled "If Wishes Were _____."

Taking It Further . . .

Children can illustrate their animal adventures. Display the pictures beside each student's story or poem on a bulletin board entitled "If Wishes Were . . . ." Have each student write the name of his or her animal in large block letters and mount the letters beside the story and illustration.

If Wishes Were Horses

WRITING CLASSIFIED ADS

Materials:

- classified ads
- lined paper
- pencils

Lesson Procedure

1. Reread the rhyme that describes criteria for buying a horse based on how many white feet it has.
2. Invite students to think of criteria they would consider before buying a horse. Students might suggest age, physical condition, training, spirit, and responsiveness. List student ideas on the chalkboard.
3. Encourage students to browse through the classified ads section of a newspaper. Point out that the fee for placing such an ad is usually based on the number of words or lines the ad contains.
4. Have students write concise ads advertising the sale of an imaginary horse or a well-known horse from literature. Emphasize providing all the essential information using minimal words.

Taking It Further . . .

To encourage students to write concise descriptions, tell them that each word will cost $1.00. Challenge students to write an ad to sell their horse (or any other item) that will cost under $15.00. Assign higher prices to common or overused words, such as *and* to encourage students to think of other ways to effectively describe their items for sale.

If Wishes Were Horses

The Midnight Farm

This gentle lullaby and counting rhyme, illustrated with soft, glowing colors, transforms midnight from an intimidating mystery to a joyful discovery. Readers will realize that darkness can be celebrated rather than feared.

Written by Reeve Lindbergh
New York: Dial, 1987

☙ TALKING NUMBERS ❧

Materials:

- worksheet on page 53
- pencils

Lesson Procedure

1. Discuss the subtle integration of numbers into the poem (one old dog, two white cats, three raccoons, and so on).
2. Discuss some of the ways that numbers are integrated into our everyday lives, such as in addresses, phone numbers, money, ages, radio and TV channels, and page numbers in books.
3. Point out some common expressions that contain references to numbers.

    I think I'll catch *forty* winks.
    It broke into a *million* pieces.
    She walks *ninety* miles an hour.

4. Invite students to fill in the correct number for each sentence on the worksheet.

    Worksheet Answer Key
    1. seven
    2. thirteen
    3. Three
    4. fours
    5. One

Taking It Further . . .

Invite students to make humorous illustrations for each number expression emphasizing a literal translation. Then encourage students to write a brief interpretation of the actual meaning of each expression.

Name_____

Talking Numbers

Complete the sentences by writing the correct number in each blank. Write your own number sentences.

    One   fours   thirteen
    Three   seven

1. The crew sailed the _____ seas.

2. A "baker's dozen" equals _____.

3. _____ is a crowd.

4. He crept around the room on all _____.

5. _____ for the money.

The Midnight Farm

• DRAWING FARM ANIMALS •

Materials:

- drawing paper
- pencils

Lesson Procedure

1. Ask students to recall the farm animals mentioned in the story and make a list on the chalkboard.
2. Use the illustrations here to demonstrate how to draw animal faces.
3. Encourage children to draw their own versions of the animal faces on drawing paper.

DOG

CAT

RACOON

GOOSE

The Midnight Farm

COW

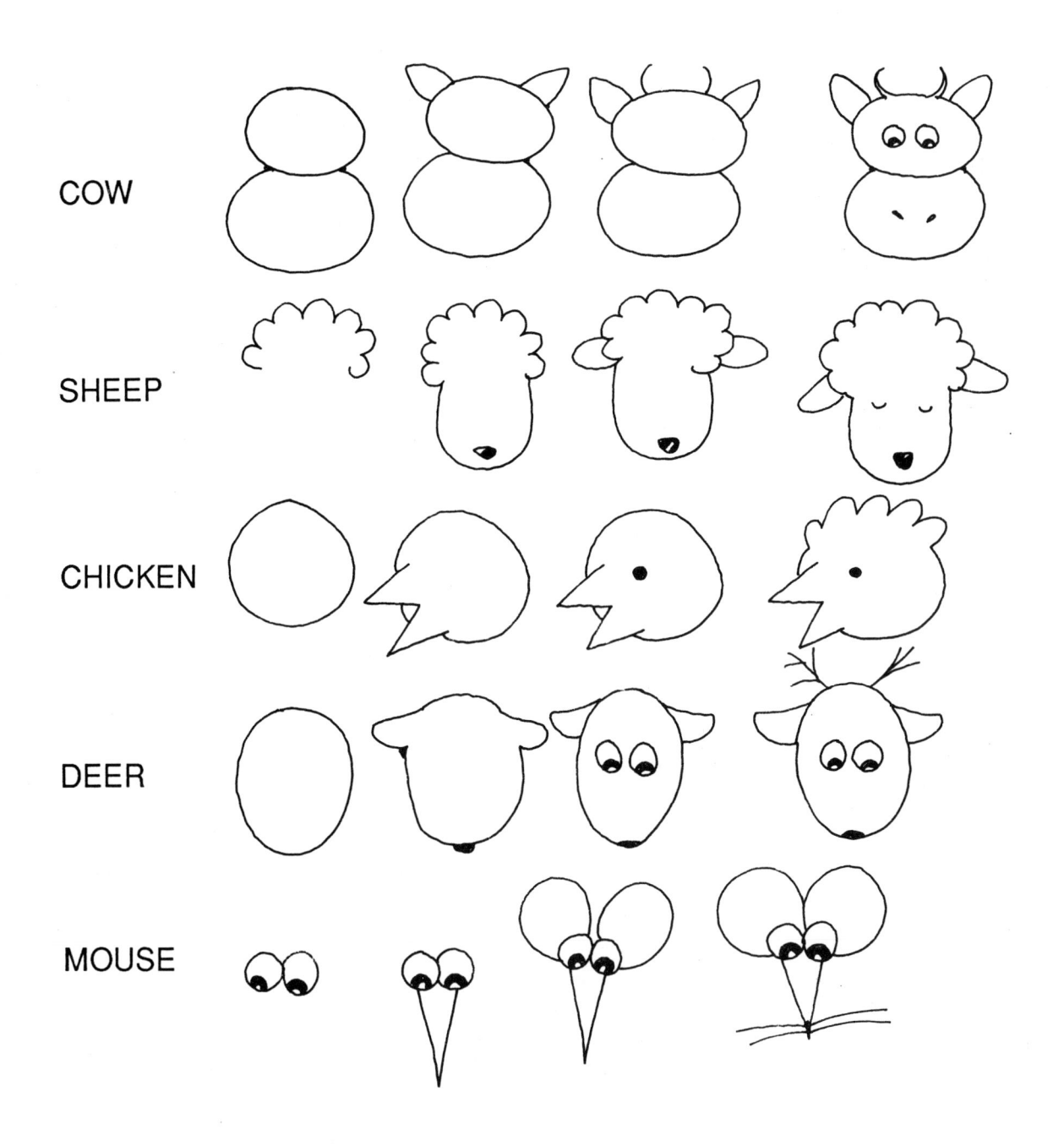

SHEEP

CHICKEN

DEER

MOUSE

The Midnight Farm

Taking It Further . . .

Students can use ½" graph paper to show the number of each animal mentioned in the story. Write the names of the animals down the left side of the paper. Have the students draw animal heads next to each animal name to represent the quantity mentioned in the story. For example, students would draw one dog, two cats, three raccoons, and so on.

Silent Night

The mystery and majesty of Christmas night are depicted in heavenly colors. The luminous blues impose a sense of wonderment, while touches of grayish-brown reassure with earthly reality. The exceptional art in this book makes it an important addition to the Susan Jeffers collection.

Written by Joseph Mohr
New York: Dutton, 1984

• DARK AND LIGHT •

Materials:

- worksheets on pages 59-60
- pencils
- butcher paper
- slide projector or spotlight
- mirrors
- small bowl
- clear drinking glass
- wax paper, tissue paper, cardboard, sheer fabric
- flashlights

Lesson Procedure

1. Although the story's setting is in the dark of night, the illustrator illuminates parts of each picture with a warm glow to add focus. Reread the story and invite children to pay special attention to the use of light in Susan Jeffers' illustrations. Point out the twinkling stars, the shadows cast by the animals, the candles, and the beams of light streaming in through windows.
2. Discuss some characteristics of or interesting facts about light.

    Light travels at 186,000 miles per second through air.
    White light is really a mixture of colors. It is made up of red, orange, yellow, green, blue, indigo, and violet.
    The sun is 94 million miles from Earth. It takes sunlight eight minutes to reach us.

3. Explain to students that they will be discovering some amazing characteristics of light while working in cooperative-learning groups and conducting several science experiments. Divide the class into small work-station groups and give each student a copy of the worksheets. Invite groups to conduct each experiment and draw some conclusions.

Taking It Further . . .

Stimulate your students to find out more about light. *Bouncing and Bending Light* (New York: Franklin Watts, 1990) is an excellent source of fun facts and experiments.

Name _____

Experiments with Light

1. Light Can Travel in a Straight Line

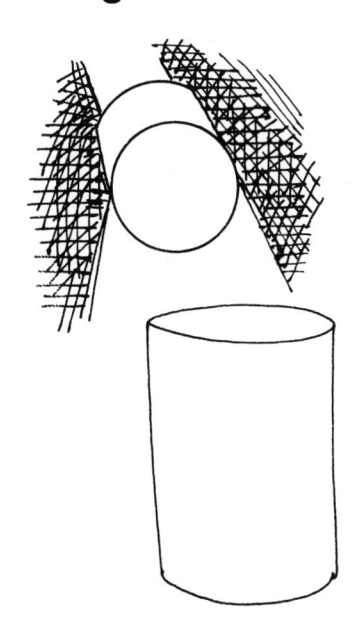

You will need:

- spotlight
- butcher paper
- tape
- pencils

Except under certain conditions in which light is refracted (when light bends as it goes through certain materials), light does not bend around objects. It travels in a straight line. If light hits an object that will not let the light through, a shadow forms behind the object.

Tape the butcher paper to a wall. Shine the spotlight on the paper. Hold your hand or any object in front of the light to cast a shadow. Trace the shadow on the paper.

Think: What causes a shadow?

2. Light Bounces Back

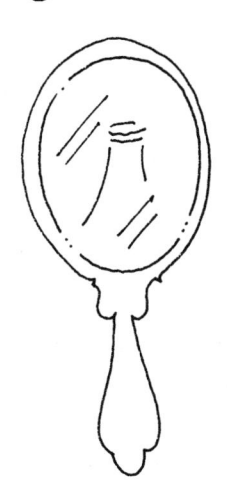

You will need:

- mirror

When light hits a surface, it bounces back. The light waves are reflected. If the surface or object is transparent, some of the light waves pass through the object. When light hits a surface at a certain angle, it always bounces off at a matching angle. Use a mirror to reflect light onto different objects.

Think: What happens when light is reflected to an object close by? To an object farther away?

Silent Night

3. Light Can Bend

You will need:

- pencils
- transparent drinking glass
- water
- paper

Rays of light actually change direction or bend when they pass through different kinds of transparent materials. This is because light travels through different transparent materials at different speeds. For example, light travels more slowly through glass or water than it does through air. When the light bends, it is called *refraction*.

Put a pencil in an empty drinking glass. Look at the pencil from the side of the glass. Does the pencil look straight? Now fill the glass half full with water. Put the pencil in the water. Look at the pencil from the side of the glass. Does the pencil look straight? The light waves must travel through the water. The water causes the light waves to bend.

Write your name on a piece of paper. Stand the paper behind the glass of water. Look at your name through the glass. How does it look?

Think: What happens to your name? Why? _____

_____

4. Light Travels Through Many Materials

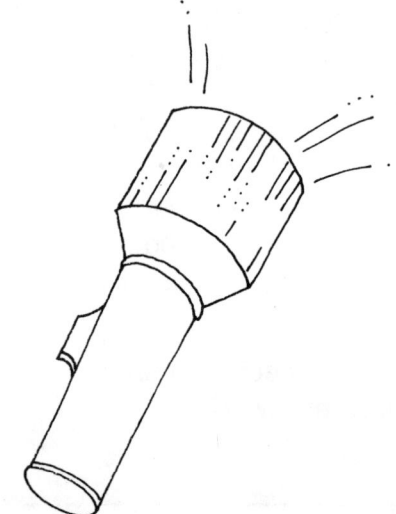

You will need:

- flashlight
- wax paper
- tissue paper
- cardboard
- fabric

Materials that block out light are called *opaque*. Materials that allow light to pass through are called *transparent*. Using the flashlight, shine light towards several types of materials. Which materials are opaque? Which materials are transparent? Some transparent materials allow more light to shine through than others. List the materials in order of how much light they let through from least to most.

Think: Will light shine through your hand? Why or why not? _____

_____

Silent Night

The Snow Queen

Andersen's haunting tale of good and evil, love and hate, summer and winter is brilliantly interpreted through Susan Jeffers' exquisite art. Text and art merge to create an engaging winter world.

Written by Hans Christian Andersen
and retold by Amy Ehrlich
New York: Dial, 1982

PROPERTIES OF WATER

Materials:

- worksheet on page 63
- pencils
- glass bowl
- small bottle
- food coloring
- clear, plastic drinking cup
- ice cubes
- sauce pan and hot plate or electric teapot
- paper towels

Lesson Procedure

1. There are many references to water and its various forms throughout the story. Invite children to recall those parts of the story and make a list on the chalkboard.

Solid	Liquid	Gas
ice on windows	melted the ice with a hot copper coin	Gerda's breath formed vapor in the frozen air
Snow Queen made of glittering ice	river	
piece of ice to cool reindeer's head	tears	
snowflakes		
palace walls		

2. Discuss how it is possible to change the state of water from liquid to solid to gas.
3. Divide the class into groups of four. Give each group a worksheet. Explain to students that they will be making some interesting discoveries about water as they read and follow the directions for the science experiments.

Taking It Further . . .

Have an ice cube melting contest. Give each student an ice cube in a paper cup. Challenge students to devise ways to make their ice cube melt the slowest or the fastest.

The Snow Queen

Name _____

Properties of Water

1. Is Water Always Wet?

What you need:
- paper towels
- bowl of water
- ice cube

Touch a paper towel to a bowl of water. Touch another paper towel to an ice cube. Did both towels get wet? Why or why not?

_____
_____

2. Is Some Water Heavier Than Other Water?

What you need:
- clear bowl of warm water
- small bottle filled with cold water
- food coloring

Add a few drops of food coloring to the cold water in the bottle. Hold your thumb over the opening to the bottle to seal it. Lower the bottle into the bowl of warm water. Release your thumb from the bottle. What happens to the cold (colored) water? Why? Try the experiment again, filling the bowl with cold water and the bottle with warm water. What happens?

_____
_____

3. Does Water Grow?

What you need:
- clear, plastic-drinking cup
- water
- permanent marker

Fill the cup 3/4 full of water. Mark the water level on the side of the cup. Put the cup into a freezer. After the water has turned to ice, check the water level. Is the water level the same? Why or why not?

_____
_____

The Snow Queen

CRYSTAL PALACES

Materials:

- construction paper (blue and black)
- crayons (white, yellow, and pink)
- salt-water solution (1 part Epsom salt and 1 part water)
- paintbrushes

Lesson Procedure

1. Ask children to describe the Snow Queen's palace. Remind them of the glittering walls of ice.
2. Using light-colored crayons, have students draw palaces on dark construction paper.
3. After the drawings are complete, have students brush over their drawings with the salt-water solution. Set the pictures aside to dry. When the salt-water solution dries, the palaces will be covered with beautiful crystals.

Taking It Further . . .

Students might enjoy learning more fascinating facts about crystals. For example, crystals are solids whose atoms are arranged in a repeating, orderly pattern. Metals, rocks, snowflakes, salt, and sugar are all made up of crystals. Crystals have symmetrical surfaces. And, there are seven general systems of crystallization—cubic, tetragonal, hexagonal, rhombohedral, orthorhombic, monoclinic, and triclinic. Challenge students to research crystals and find out more information about them.

The Snow Queen

Snow White and the Seven Dwarfs

This familiar fairy tale is retold and illustrated with simplicity and charm. Susan Jeffers' animals are alluring, her dwarfs winsome, and her wicked queen wonderfully vain. Children will want to return to this enchanting version again and again.

Retold by Freya Littledale
New York: Scholastic, 1980

USING THE YELLOW PAGES

Materials:

- worksheets on pages 67-68
- yellow pages phone book
- pencils

Lesson Procedure

1. The story suggests several reasons why the characters might need to consult the yellow pages. For example, Snow White could have "let her fingers do the walking" to find help for cleaning the dwarfs' house. Or, the queen could have found where to buy a mirror to admire herself by looking for glass companies in the phone book. Invite children to suggest other scenarios in which the characters would have found the yellow pages helpful.
2. Discuss how to determine major headings and how to use guide words to locate listings. Divide the class into groups of 2-4 students, and have them use the yellow pages to complete the worksheets.

Taking It Further . . .

Invite students to recall an ad they noticed as they browsed through the yellow pages that particularly caught their attention. Ask students to define what makes that ad attractive and appealing to them. Encourage students to design their own ads using principles of good design.

Snow White and the Seven Dwarfs

Name _____

Using the Yellow Pages

Carefully read and follow the directions to help the characters from *Snow White and the Seven Dwarfs* find the assistance they need.

1. Snow White decides to get help cleaning the dwarfs' house. Look up "House Cleaning" in the yellow pages.

    What are the guide words at the top of the pages? _____
    _____

    List three agencies that clean houses.

    _____
    _____
    _____
    _____

2. The queen decides to get a new mirror. Look up "Glass" in the yellow pages.

    What are the guide words at the top of the pages? _____
    _____

    List three entries that sell mirrors.

    _____
    _____
    _____
    _____

3. The dwarfs need to order a new bed that will be the right size for Snow White. Look up "Furniture" in the yellow pages.

    What are the guide words at the top of the pages? _____
    _____

    List three furniture store entries.

    _____
    _____
    _____
    _____

Snow White and the Seven Dwarfs

4. Snow White needs to know where she can buy enough bread to feed all of the dwarfs. She wants to call a baker. Look up "Bakers" in the yellow pages.

    What are the guide words at the top of the pages? _____

    _____

    List three bakers.

    _____

    _____

    _____

5. The queen wants to find the very best-looking apple to trick Snow White. Look up "Produce," "Fruit," or "Grocer" in the yellow pages.

    What are the guide words at the top of the pages? _____

    _____

    List three entries.

    _____

    _____

    _____

6. The prince wants to hire the best wedding caterer for the royal wedding. Look up "Wedding Services" in the yellow pages.

    What are the guide words at the top of the pages? _____

    _____

    List three wedding service listings.

    _____

    _____

    _____

Snow White and the Seven Dwarfs

STRANGER AWARENESS

Materials:

- worksheet on page 70
- pencils
- crayons, markers, or colored pencils

Lesson Procedure

1. Snow White was confronted by a stranger several times throughout the story. She made some mistakes dealing with the situations that ended up causing her harm. Ask students what mistakes they think Snow White made. Encourage students to tell how they would have handled the situations had they been in Snow White's place.

2. Ask students to name safety rules to remember when they come in contact with a stranger. List the ideas on the chalkboard. Your list might include:

   Do not talk to strangers.
   Do not give out information to strangers.
   Do not tell a stranger on the phone that you are home alone.
   Know who you can call for help if trouble arises.

3. Invite each student to choose one safety rule from the list and design a poster on the apple worksheet.

Taking It Further . . .

Display the apple posters around your classroom or throughout your school. Encourage students to choose a partner and work out a short skit demonstrating one of the safety rules. Invite pairs to perform the skit for the class. Role-playing will help students visualize and internalize the messages.

Snow White and the Seven Dwarfs

Name _____

Snow White and the Seven Dwarfs

Stopping by Woods on a Snowy Evening

One of America's most well-known poems is quietly interpreted by one of children's literature's most talented artists. The black and white pictures, with just a touch of color, beautifully contrast the frozen stillness of winter with the warmth of the moment. The miracle of capturing one instant of time, so skillfully penned by Robert Frost, is again caught by Susan Jeffers' brush.

Written by Robert Frost
New York: Dutton, 1978

ADJECTIVE SNOWFLAKES

Materials:

- worksheet on page 73
- pencils
- tracing paper
- drawing paper

Lesson Procedure

1. Ask students to brainstorm a list of adjectives that describe snow and then list the adjectives on the chalkboard.
2. Direct each student to choose one adjective from the list. On a piece of scratch paper, encourage students to experiment writing their chosen words with various styles and sizes of handwriting. Encourage creativity.
3. Give each student a copy of the worksheet. Ask students to make an adjective snowflake by writing their chosen adjectives on each line of a "snowflake skeleton." Remind students to rotate the snowflake the same direction as they write the word each time.
4. Encourage students to choose other adjectives to complete each "snowflake skeleton" on the worksheet.
5. Using a piece of drawing paper, have students trace over their adjective snowflakes, omitting the skeleton lines. Students can trace several adjective snowflakes on the same piece of paper to create an "adjective snowstorm." Each word and lettering style will create a unique design, just as every snowflake has its unique structure.

Taking It Further . . .

Encourage students to use adjectives from their "adjective snowstorms" to write a story or poem. Mount each student's story and snowstorm side by side on a 12" x 18" piece of black construction paper.

Name _____

Adjective Snowflakes

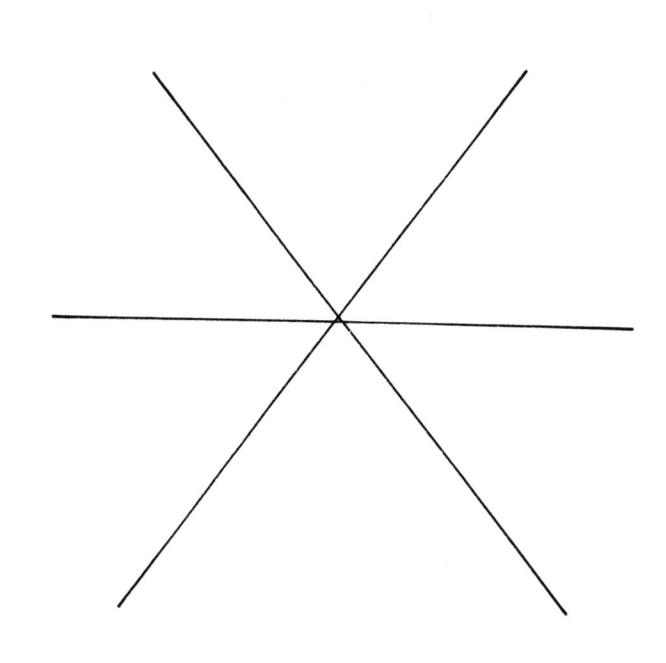

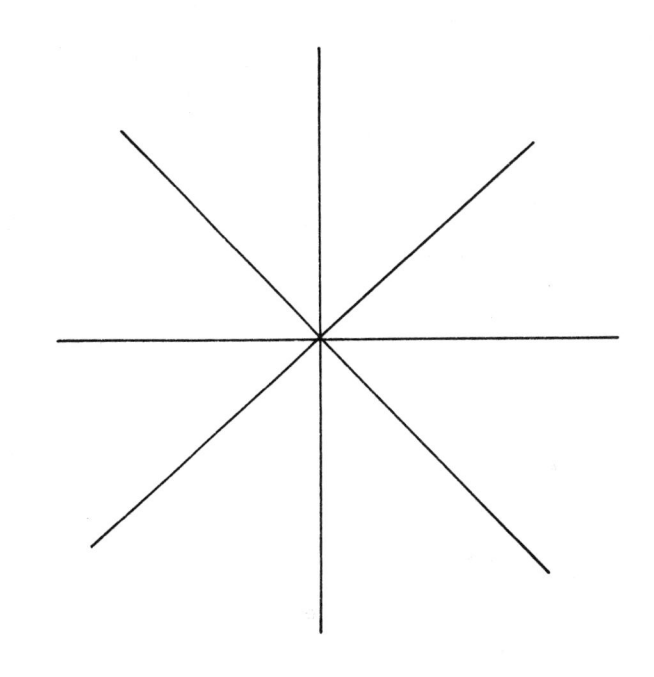

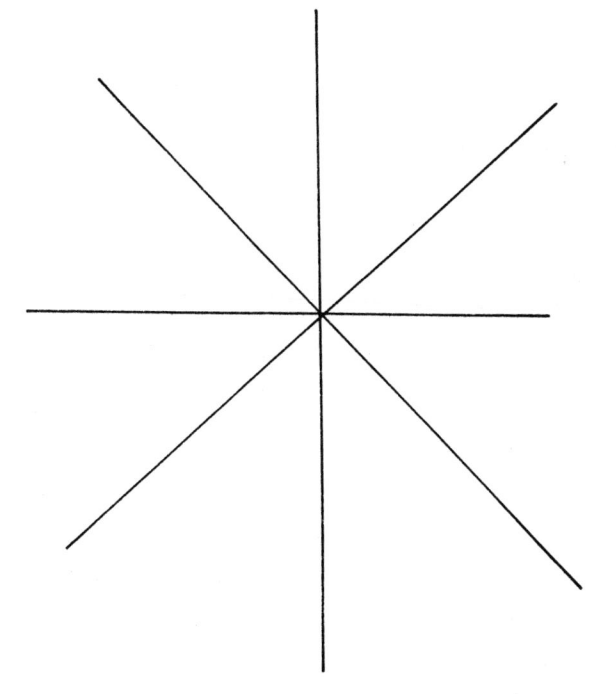

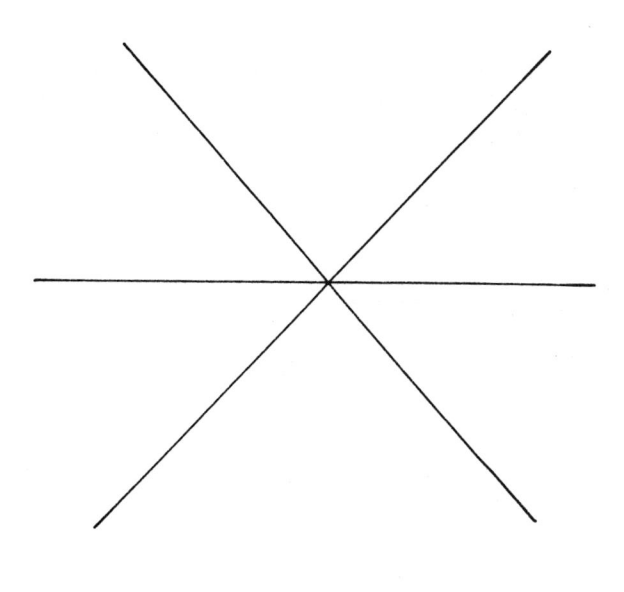

Stopping by Woods on a Snowy Evening

73

• SNOWFLAKE ORIGINALS •

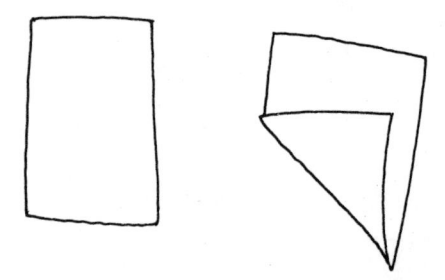

Materials:

- drawing paper
- rulers
- pencils
- scissors

Lesson Procedure

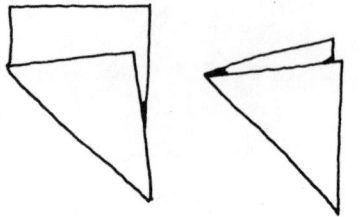

1. Lay paper vertically on a desk or table. Fold the bottom edge over to one side to form a triangle.

2. Cut off the rectangular flap extending above the triangle.

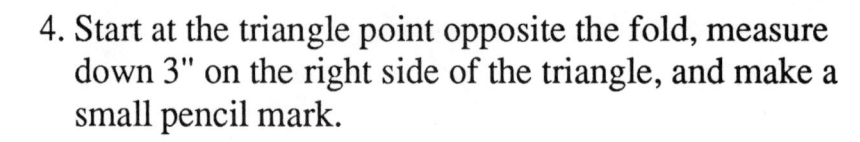

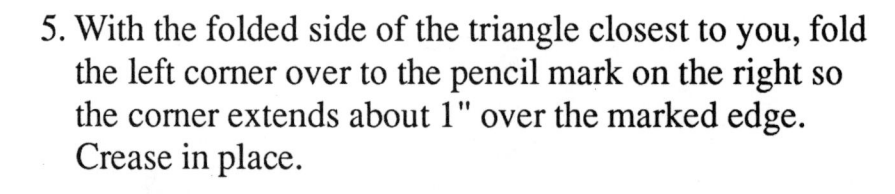

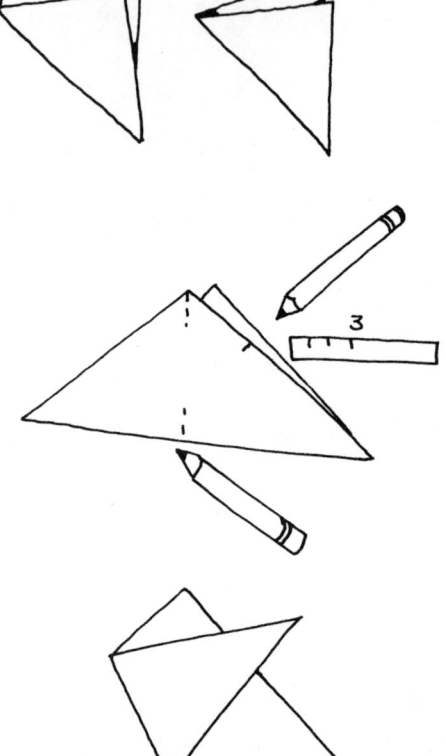

3. Find the center of the folded edge of the triangle by folding it in half and making a small crease. Unfold.

4. Start at the triangle point opposite the fold, measure down 3" on the right side of the triangle, and make a small pencil mark.

5. With the folded side of the triangle closest to you, fold the left corner over to the pencil mark on the right so the corner extends about 1" over the marked edge. Crease in place.

Stopping by Woods on a Snowy Evening

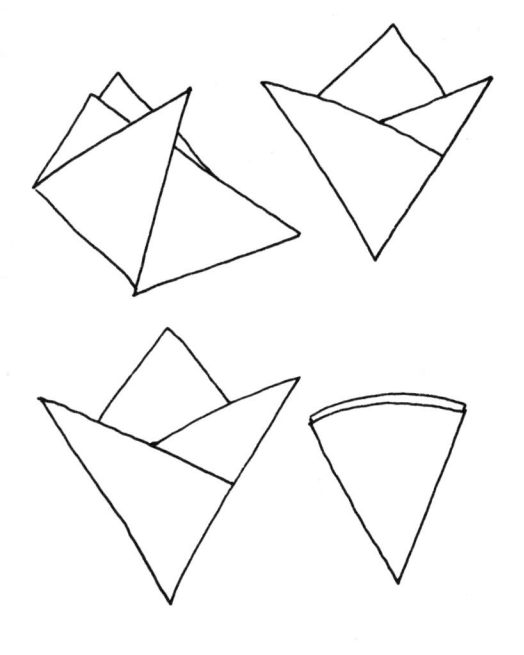

6. Fold the right corner toward the left side so it overlaps in the same way.

7. Using scissors, round the top edges to create a cone shape.

8. Without cutting completely up either folded side, cut designs into both sides and the top.

9. Unfold the paper to reveal a beautiful and unique snowflake.

Taking It Further . . .

Invite students to experiment with hole punchers to create interesting designs in their snowflakes.

Stopping by Woods on a Snowy Evening

The Three Jovial Huntsmen

The animals hiding among the bushes and trees in the woods snicker as the three jovial huntsmen pass by unaware. Susan Jeffers' illustrations superbly capture the merriment of this seemingly unsuccessful hunting trip as the reader enjoys the antics of these three silly fellows.

New York: Bradbury Press, 1973

PATTERNED WRITING

Materials:

- worksheet on page 79
- pencils

Lesson Procedure

1. Discuss some of the things the three jovial huntsmen saw in the woods and what they actually thought the objects were.

   a rock looked like a ship or a house with the chimney blown away
   the moon looked like a piece of cheese
   a hedgehog looked like a pincushion
   skunk tails looked like a hare's ears

2. Reread the story and ask children to pay special attention to the pattern used to describe each object the hunters saw.

3. Choose an object in the classroom and invite students to imagine that the three hunters have found it. Ask students to describe the object from the hunters' point of view. Choose a student to draw the object on the chalkboard.

   All the day they hunted,
   And nothing could they find,
   But a <u>pencil a-rolling</u>,
   And that they left behind.

   The first said it was a <u>pencil</u>,
   The second he said, Nay,
   The third said it was a <u>rocket</u>
   <u>A flying on its way</u>.

4. Challenge students to write their own verses on the worksheet.

Taking It Further . . .

Show the class an interesting picture from a magazine or a book. Invite volunteers to describe what they see in the picture from different points of view.

   A boy said it was . . .
   A worm said it was . . .
   A bird said it was . . .

The Three Jovial Huntsmen

Name _____

Jovial Hunting

All the day they hunted,
And nothing could they find,
But a _____ _____,
       (noun)   (verb)
And that they left behind.

The first said it was a _____,
The second he said, Nay,   (repeat noun)
The third said it was a _____
                            (noun)
_____.
            (action of noun)

The Three Jovial Huntsmen

79

HIDDEN PICTURES

Materials:

- drawing paper
- pencils
- black crayons or felt-tip markers

Lesson Procedure

1. Remind students how, in the story, the three jovial huntsmen imagined objects to be something other than what they really were. Their imaginations conjured up some unrealistic images.
2. Have each student create a simple, abstract scribble on a sheet of drawing paper using a black crayon or marker.
3. Have students exchange scribbles with other classmates. Encourage students to let their imaginations run wild and transform the abstract scribbles into something concrete by adding eyes, feet, hair, wheels, or other details.

Taking It Further . . .

Encourage students to write paragraphs or short stories about their scribble designs.

The Three Jovial Huntsmen

Thumbelina

Thumbelina, no larger than the size of a thumb, soon discovers that the natural world is one of giant creatures, towering plants, and overwhelming adventures. Susan Jeffers' illustrations easily draw the reader into this giant world as viewed from Thumbelina's miniature perspective.

Written by Hans Christian Andersen
and retold by Amy Ehrlich
New York: Dial, 1979

MINIATURE MAGIC

Materials:

- worksheet on page 83
- pencils

Lesson Procedure

1. Discuss some of the problems Thumbelina faced because she was so small. Discuss the advantages and disadvantages of being no larger than a thumb.
2. Invite children to imagine what it would be like if they magically became as small as Thumbelina. Encourage students to think of scenarios in their typical day that would become embarrassing, funny, difficult, or impossible because of their new miniature size.
3. Give each student a copy of the worksheet. Invite girls to think of themselves as Thumbelina and boys to think of themselves as Thumbert. Encourage students to write about their miniature adventures.

Taking It Further . . .

After editing the stories, students can recopy them into miniature booklets and add illustrations.

Thumbelina

Name _____

Miniature Magic

Imagine that by some mysterious magic you have been turned into a miniature person for the day. Write about your adventures.

FOUR SEASONS

Materials:

- worksheet on page 85
- pencils

Lesson Procedure

1. Ask students in what season of the year the story begins (spring or early summer). Reread the story and encourage students to point out each mention of the seasons as the story unfolds.

   "The whole summer through Thumbelina lived by herself . . ."
   "But when summer ended, the plants and flowers withered."
   "Autumn passed, and then one day it began to snow."
   "When spring warmed the earth once more . . ."
   "Summer was ending . . ."
   ". . . the mole and the field mouse agreed that she would be married to him in the autumn."
   "The cold winter is coming again."

2. Ask students how long the span of time was from the beginning of the story to the end (two years). Invite students to use the worksheet to list some seasonal changes that happen throughout the year. Students can list ways animals' habits change, plants change, or their own habits change. Use examples from the story.

   leaves turn brown and wither in winter
   dry corn smell fills the winter air
   field mice spend the winter in underground burrows
   birds migrate in autumn and spring

Taking It Further . . .

Invite students to look more closely at the beautiful leaves Susan Jeffers has illustrated. Make leaf print stationery. Fold a piece of drawing paper in half. Paint one side of a green, pliable leaf with tempera paint. Press the front cover of the folded stationery over the painted leaf to make a print.

Name _____

List some changes you notice in plants, animals, or yourself during each season of the year.

FOUR SEASONS

Spring _____
_____
_____

Summer _____
_____
_____

Fall _____
_____
_____

Winter _____
_____
_____

Thumbelina

• WALNUT SHELL ART •

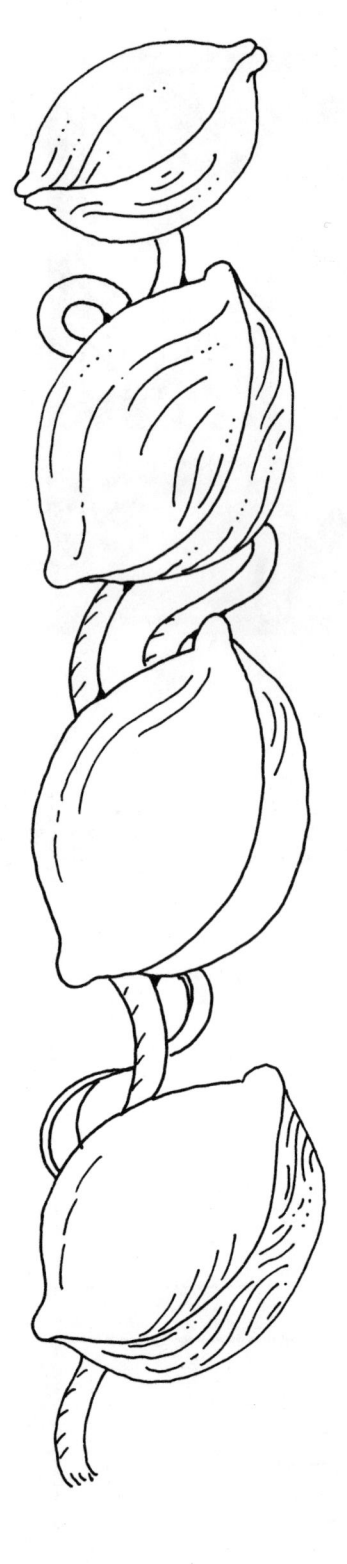

Materials:

- walnut shell halves
- construction paper (assorted colors)
- yarn
- scissors
- glue
- crayons or felt-tip markers

Lesson Procedure

1. Discuss Thumbelina's walnut shell bed. Ask students to imagine other ways Thumbelina could have used a walnut shell, such as for a sled, wagon, or bathtub.
2. Give each student a walnut shell and ask students to think of some creative ways to use it.
3. Encourage students to think of something they could make out of the walnut shell using the provided art supplies.

Taking It Further . . .

Invite students to make a miniature house for Thumbelina. Students could use shoeboxes for rooms and make miniature furniture out of walnut shells, empty thread spools, or match boxes.

Thumbelina

Wild

Susan Jeffers has skillfully interpreted the Scottish ballad of "Tamlane" in terms young children can enjoy. A wild, unruly boy runs away and is captured by fairies. His sister, Janet, must free him from the fairy spell. Rich, transparent colors recreate the magical world beyond the moors.

New York: Dutton, 1976

Robin

CREATIVE WRITING

Materials:

- lined paper
- pencils

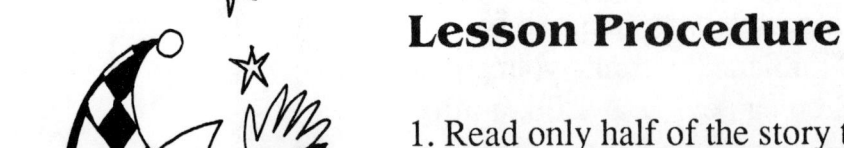

Lesson Procedure

1. Read only half of the story to the students. Stop reading after the elf shows Janet her brother in a dream—"And Robin told her how she could free him." Remind students that good stories contain a conflict that must be solved. Invite students to think of solutions to the conflict presented in this story. Encourage students to suggest ways Janet could save her brother from the Queen.
2. Have students write down their suggestions and then share them with the class.
3. Finish reading the book. Compare student solutions with the solutions presented in the story.

Taking It Further . . .

Read *Tam Lin* by Jane Yolen and illustrated by Charles Mikolaycak (San Diego: Harcourt, Brace, and Jovanovich, 1990) which is another version of the same story. Invite students to make comparisons between the two stories.

The Wild Swans

One of Andersen's most powerful tales is eloquently recreated in bold, exquisite paintings. The well-known story of a young girl setting out to rescue her eleven brothers who have been turned into swans is powerfully brought to life by Susan Jeffers' magnificent illustrations.

Written by Hans Christian Andersen
and retold by Amy Ehrlich
New York: Dial, 1981

CHARACTER STUDY

Materials:

- worksheet on page 91
- pencils
- lined paper

Lesson Procedure

1. Discuss the characters in the story. Ask students to identify some of the characters' attributes based on their actions and feelings.

    Elise showed her unselfishness by sacrificing her own comfort in order to free her brothers.
    The king showed consideration for Elise's feelings by making her chamber look exactly like the cavern in which she had been working.
    The youngest brother showed his compassion by weeping at the sight of Elise's blistered hands.

2. Encourage students to imagine how these same characters would react in modern-day situations based on their attributes. For example, ask students which character they would most like to be friends with, which character they think would make the best class president, and so on.
3. Give each student a worksheet and encourage children to answer the questions using imaginative and creative thinking.

Taking It Further . . .

The brothers were swans by day and humans by night. This theme of being one form by day and another by night is common in literature throughout the centuries. Invite students to create original characters who change form at night. Encourage students to write stories about their new characters.

The Wild Swans

Name _____

Character Study

Choose from the characters in *The Wild Swans* to answer each question.

Elise   wicked queen   king

youngest brother   archbishop

1. With which character would you *least* like to be stranded on a desert island? Why?
   _____
   _____

2. With which character would you *most* like to have lunch? Why? _____
   _____
   _____

3. Which character is most like you? Why?
   _____
   _____

4. Think of an occupation, such as a firefighter, teacher, or police chief, that suits each character based on his or her personal characteristics.

   Elise _____

   king _____

   archbishop _____

   youngest brother _____

   wicked queen _____

The Wild Swans

• PLANTS •

Materials:

- science texts
- wildflower field guides
- drawing paper
- lined paper
- pencils
- crayons, markers, or colored pencils

Lesson Procedure

1. Discuss Susan Jeffers' attention to botanical detail. Several plants are named in the text (red poppies, willow bark and rushes, nettle, and roses), while others are accurately illustrated.
2. Set up a center in your classroom complete with the materials listed above and a copy or two of *The Wild Swans*.
3. Encourage students to use the reference books to identify some of the plants illustrated by Susan Jeffers in the story.
4. Students can draw a picture of the plant, label the plant, and identify the page of the book on which it is illustrated.
5. Invite students to write the name of the plant they chose on lined paper and then write three facts they learned about it.
6. Display the completed work on a bulletin board near the center.

Taking It Further . . .

Challenge the students to locate specimens of the plants. Encourage the students to draw pictures of the specimens in their natural environment. Caution students not to disturb the environment around their plant specimen.

Wynken, Blynken, and Nod

Illustrated in flat colors and bold shapes, this version of the well-loved poem will charm children of any age. The spellbinding language will capture eager adventurers and carry readers comfortably into a world of bedtime images.

Written by Eugene Field
New York: Dutton, 1982

• NIGHT WRITERS •

Materials:

- worksheet on page 95
- pencils

Lesson Procedure

1. Explain to students what a metaphor is and give some examples.

    A metaphor is an implied comparison between two usually unrelated things. A metaphor does not use the words "like" or "as" to make the comparison.

2. Ask children to recall some of the metaphors used in the book *Wynken, Blynken, and Nod*.

    stars are fish
    bed is a boat
    sky is the sea

3. Invite students to write their own nighttime adventures on the worksheet provided. Encourage students to make creative comparisons for the moon, stars, darkness, sky, and night noises.

Taking It Further . . .

Point out the various shades of blue Susan Jeffers uses in her illustrations. Challenge students to choose one color and use various shades to illustrate their stories.

Wynken, Blynken, and Nod

Name _____

Riding into the Night . . .

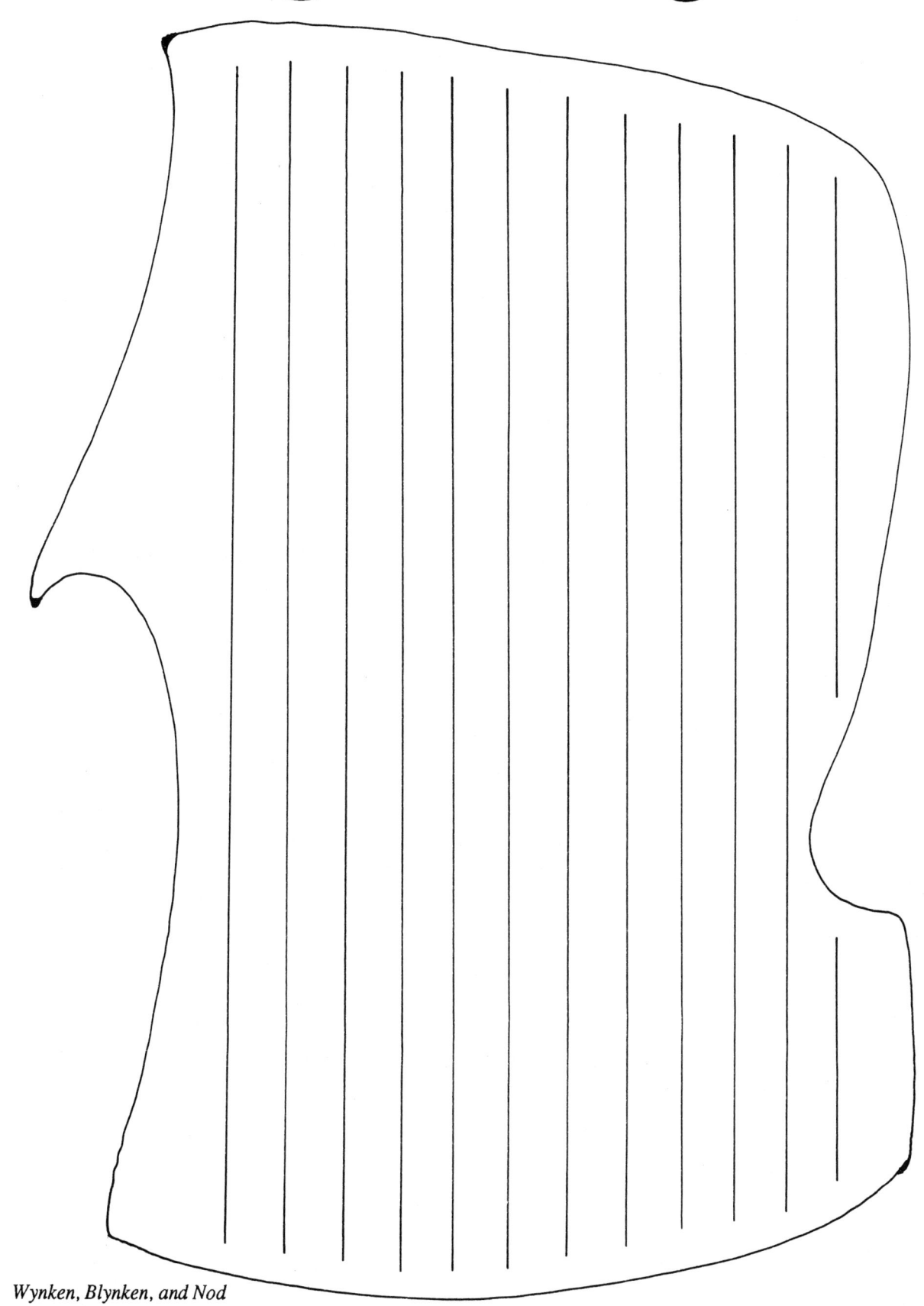

Wynken, Blynken, and Nod

CML Text LB1043 H694 1992
Howell, Will C
The Susan Jeffers
connection

**NO LONGER THE PROPERTY
OF THE
UNIVERSITY OF R.I. LIBRARY**